The "Faith in Action" Series
General Editors: Geoffrey Hanks and
David Wallington

THE GREAT DOCTOR

THE STORY OF ALBERT SCHWEITZER

Nancy Martin

GW00808979

RMEP

RELIGIOUS AND MORAL EDUCATION PRESS

An Imprint of Arnold-Wheaton

Religious and Moral Education Press
An Imprint of Arnold-Wheaton
Hennock Road, Exeter EX2 8RP

Pergamon Press Ltd
Headington Hill Hall, Oxford OX3 0BW

Pergamon Press Inc.
Maxwell House, Fairview Park, Elmsford, New York 10523

Pergamon Press Canada Ltd
Suite 104, 150 Consumers Road, Willowdale, Ontario M2J 1P9.

Pergamon Press (Australia) Pty Ltd
P.O. Box 544, Potts Point, N.S.W. 2011

Pergamon Press GmbH
Hammerweg 6, D-6242 Kronberg,
Federal Republic of Germany

ACKNOWLEDGEMENTS: Photographs are reproduced by courtesy of
Harold E. Robles, Secretary-General, A.I.S.L. Cover photograph by
courtesy of Popperfoto.

First published 1978
Reprinted 1979, 1983

Printed in Great Britain by A. Wheaton & Co. Ltd, Exeter

ISBN 0 08 022214 5 non net
ISBN 0 08 022215 3 net

THE GREAT DOCTOR

The story of Albert Schweitzer

"Go it, George. Keep your end up. Don't let young Albert get you down."

George was beginning to look angry as his schoolboy friends shouted at him. He knew he was getting the worst of the fight. Albert came at him again and again, trying to throw him to the ground. George could not shake him off.

The boys who were looking on groaned as George went down. Albert stood over him.

"If I had good food to eat like you get I'd be as strong as you," grumbled George.

"You're right, George," said one of his friends. "He's better off than we are."

Those words bothered Albert Schweitzer. Just because he was a parson's son the other boys thought he was different from them. He did not want to be different, so he tried not to be. They did not wear overcoats, so he would not do so. They wore wooden clogs instead of shoes, and caps which they pulled down over their ears. He would do the same. His mother was cross with him, but he felt he had to be like the other boys.

Albert was a dreamy boy with a love of nature and a great feeling for animals. He could not forget seeing an old horse being beaten as it was dragged through the streets to the knacker's yard to be killed. All through his life he cared for all living things, trying to protect them whenever he could. He called it "reverence for life".

But his wish to be like the other boys sometimes led him to do things which he knew were wrong. One day he and one of his friends each made a catapult.

"Come on," said his friend, Henry. "Let's go and shoot some birds."

Albert did not have the courage to refuse for fear of being laughed at. But he felt bad about it, especially when he heard the birds singing in the woods.

Henry put a stone in his catapult and nodded to Albert to do the same. It was very quiet as they took aim. Then the church bells began to ring. Albert dropped his catapult and raced for home, while the birds flew away. He felt that the bells were a warning to him. For the rest of his life he tried to stick to what he felt to be right, no matter what others thought of him.

All this happened in Gunsbach, where Albert's father was the parson. They had moved to the village soon after Albert was born, in January 1875. It was a small village set in a valley among the lovely mountains of Alsace. This area is now part of France, but then it was under German rule.

In church Albert loved the music. He learned to play the organ as soon as his feet could reach the pedals. By the time he was ten he was playing for some of the services in the village church. In fact, he was showing signs of becoming a great organist.

At the Sunday afternoon services his father read letters from missionaries who were working and teaching in Africa. These letters made him think about the people of that country. He knew that a law had been passed by France forbidding the sale of Africans as slaves. This was in

1848, only twenty-seven years before Albert was born. It had been a hard fight because white people in other countries wanted Africans as cheap labour.

Although the Africans were free from slavery they were not yet free from fear. They lived in terror of evil spirits. They suffered from many diseases. Often they were attacked by wild animals, or bitten by poisonous snakes. Yet they had no doctor except the witch-doctor. He sold them fetishes, or charms, to drive out the evil spirits. Some were just small bags of feathers, or bones. If the patient did not get better he had to buy a bigger and more costly fetish. This might be the skull of someone who had been killed simply for this purpose.

People who were mentally ill were often bound and thrown into the river. Nobody, not even the witch-doctors, knew what to do with them.

Everyone was under the power of these so-called

Schweitzer at his desk in Lambarene, about 1935

"doctors". When a mother gave birth to a baby, her face and the baby's were painted white to scare away the evil spirits.

These were the things which happened when Albert was a boy. Such news from far-away Africa made him sad. He wanted to teach these people a better way.

" I know what I must do"

At the age of eighteen Albert went to Strasbourg University to study to be a parson like his father. He also studied music. He met some of the famous composers of the day. He also wrote a book about Bach, who had lived about 200 years earlier, and who composed some great organ music. This book is still one of the best which has been written about him.

Schweitzer himself was now becoming well known. He was often invited to play at concerts and give talks on music and his beliefs about God.

He did some social work among neglected children, and did what he could to help men who were tramps or homeless. But he always felt that this was not what he was really called to do.

When he gave up doing this he spent all day and much of the night at his studies. He wrote books on the subjects he was studying. But his feeling for the suffering Africans became so great that he knew he must one day do something to help them. He made up his mind to go on with his studies until he was thirty. Then he would give the rest of his life to the service of others.

He passed his final exams, and two years later, at the age of twenty-eight, he became Principal of his college.

One day he happened to read an article about the needs of the Congo Mission. This made him think about Africa again. The article described Gabon, a country in West

4

West Coast of Africa
showing position of Gabon

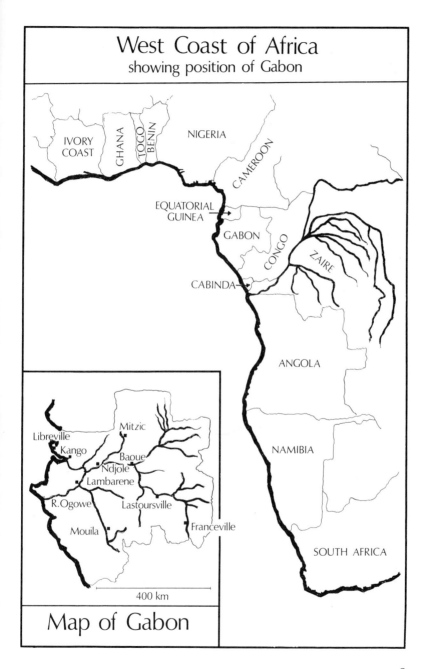

IVORY
COAST

GHANA

TOGO

BENIN

NIGERIA

CAMEROON

EQUATORIAL
GUINEA

GABON

CONGO

ZAIRE

CABINDA

ANGOLA

NAMIBIA

SOUTH AFRICA

Mitzic

Libreville

Kango

Baoue

Ndjole

Lambarene

R.Ogowe

Lastoursville

Mouila

Franceville

400 km

Map of Gabon

Africa right on the equator, near the Congo. It told of the urgent need for missionaries and doctors to teach and help the people in this area. The report ended: "Men and women who can reply simply to the Master's call and say, 'Lord, I am coming', these are the people whom the Church needs."

And Albert Schweitzer knew this was what he had to do.

He went on quietly with his work in Strasbourg, telling no one of the great decision he had made. He knew that Gabon was damp, unhealthy and dangerous. He had a great future before him at home as a musician, a speaker and an author. But these people in Africa had no doctor and no hospital, so he would go there as a doctor. To meet their need he would have to begin another long course of study, as a medical student.

In October 1905 he wrote to his parents and friends: "At the beginning of the winter term I shall enter myself as a medical student in order to go later to Africa as a doctor."

Then he gave up his position as Principal of the college. He had held this for two years.

His mother was very unhappy about it. She was proud of her son's success. She knew he could become more and more famous. He seemed to be throwing away his chances. His friends felt the same.

"Why should you be the one to go?" they asked. "Why not leave such work to others who don't have so much to give up?"

"Couldn't you do more by staying here and raising money for them?" asked others.

But Schweitzer knew what he had to do. The people of Africa needed a doctor and he must try to fill that need.

After studying for six years, Schweitzer passed his final examinations and became a doctor. He went to Paris to work in a hospital and study the kind of medicine he would need to use in Africa.

In June 1912 he returned to Strasbourg to marry Helene Bresslau. She was the daughter of a university professor. As a student she had helped him in the social work he had tried to do. She had now become a nurse in order to help him with his work in Africa.

Schweitzer told the Paris Missionary Society that he wanted to go to their mission station in Lambarene, on the Ogowe River in West Africa. He said he would need no pay, nor would he come to them for money to equip the hospital. He intended to raise what was needed by his organ playing and concerts, and by giving talks. His books, too, were beginning to earn good money.

Hospital in a chicken-house

On Good Friday, 1913, Albert and Helene Schweitzer left Germany for Africa. He was going to be the first doctor at the mission station at Lambarene. His wife was going to help him. It was the beginning of a great adventure in service for others. For years he had talked about the religion of love. Now he was going to put it into practice.

Besides their trunks and baggage, they took seventy cases of medical supplies and a piano. The ship stopped at different ports as it steamed down the north-west coast of Africa, the Gold Coast (now Ghana), and the Slave Coast (now Nigeria).

At Cape Lopez the river boat took the travellers up the River Ogowe. This river runs north of the Congo and parallel with it. Giant trees grew up from the steamy jungle along the banks, their trunks covered with brightly coloured creepers. Monkeys swung from the branches.

Now and then the boat passed a native village. Naked children stared at them from their mud huts, but there was nobody at all in some villages.

"When I came out here fifteen years ago," said a trader, "these places were full of life."

"Why are they not so now?" asked Schweitzer.

"Alcohol!" replied the trader. "White men brought it here, but the villagers drank so much of the stuff they could not work."

Towards the end of their 200-mile journey they stopped at the landing stage of Lambarene, the town which gave the mission its name. But there was yet another hour's journey by canoe. The long, narrow canoe was a tree trunk hollowed out. African boys from the mission school stood as they paddled the canoe up the stream, which branched off the main river. They sang as they moved their paddles in rhythm.

The mission station was set in a clearing in the dense forest. Schweitzer was surprised to see only a few huts. The missionaries had made ready a four-roomed bungalow for him and his wife. It stood off the ground on wooden piles to keep out insects and animals. Yet no sooner were they in their house than they saw a huge spider creeping down the wall! It was the biggest they had ever seen. Schweitzer, with his love for all living things, quietly put it outside. Later, he was to find the driver ants much more difficult to deal with.

These ants usually march at night, at the beginning and end of the rainy season. They are a little bigger than other ants, and have large heads with strong jaws almost as big as the rest of their bodies. They eat everything in their path. Beetles, frogs, rats, mice and even snakes are not safe when driver ants are on the march.

Schweitzer soon discovered that his house was on their main route. When the ants started their march, the chickens made a strange clucking sound. This woke the doctor. He had to hurry to let the chickens out of their house. If they

8

were shut in, the ants would get into their mouths and nostrils and eat them, leaving only their bones.

Helene Schweitzer took a bugle from the wall and blew it three times. This brought the men helpers running with buckets of water mixed with lysol, a sort of disinfectant. They sprinkled this round the house. These ants did not like the smell so they soon moved on. But many of the men were bitten by them. Dr Schweitzer once counted nearly fifty ants clinging to him. They bit so deeply that he could not pull them off whole, and their jaws had to be taken out afterwards.

Problems which would have been too great for many men

The hospital by the River Ogowe

began to arise. Firstly, the doctor could not understand what the natives said. The man who could have explained had not arrived. Neither had the seventy cases of medical supplies. The hospital he had expected to find ready for him had not been built. There was not even a room where he could treat the patients. He could not have them in his house for fear of spreading their diseases.

With the few medical supplies he had in his trunk, Schweitzer began his work in the courtyard outside his house.

Patients with all kinds of diseases came to him as soon as they heard that a doctor was there. They came on foot and by canoe, travelling as much as seventy miles through steamy forests and in the hot sun. Their friends and relations came to help look after them.

The heat of the sun, the flies and mosquitoes, and the sight of raw wounds on patients' bodies were hard for the doctor and his helpers to bear. Many wounds had been made worse by being coated with powder made from the bark of a tree. Some people were suffering from malaria, caused by mosquito bites. Others had been injured by wild animals. Still more suffered from leprosy or dysentery.

Many had sleeping sickness. This is caused by the bite of the tsetse fly, which is about one and a half times the size of our house fly. The tsetse fly is more harmful than the mosquito. It can bite through the thickest clothes and draw blood. Unless patients are treated quickly they have dreadful headaches and get weaker and weaker until they die. Until the arrival of Dr Schweitzer there had been no doctor to treat these people.

It was nearing the end of the rainy season when he started his work. When the rains came, towards the end of the day, all medicines, bandages and supplies had to be hurriedly moved into the house, and the patients sent home.

The doctor urgently needed a surgery where he could operate. The only possible place was a disused chicken-house! He decided to use it until he could build something better. He cleaned it, whitewashed the walls and put up shelves. There were no windows and it was very hot.

An old camp-bed served as an operating-table. Helene Schweitzer cleaned the instruments, washed bandages and helped at operations.

The work begins

One of Schweitzer's first patients was a man called Joseph. He was a cook and could speak French as well as two African languages. Schweitzer made him cook and medical helper at the hospital.

Starting at 8.30 in the morning the doctor treated thirty or forty patients a day. One man had been sleeping in his hut when a leopard bit his right arm. His friends made a twelve-hour journey by canoe to get him to the doctor. By the time he arrived his arm was badly swollen and he had a high fever. When the doctor examined him he saw four tiny pricks made by the leopard's claws. Beneath these marks the flesh had been torn away right down to the bone. After treatment he was soon well enough to return to his village. Another man was walking through the forest when he was scalped by a gorilla. He too was brought to the doctor for help. If Schweitzer had not gone to Africa these men, and very many others, would have suffered and died from such accidents.

At sunset, at six o'clock, darkness fell suddenly and many patients had to be sent away until the next day. Some turned the mission schoolboys out of their beds and slept there!

Before Schweitzer could plan his hospital he had to get permission to build. He set out with the other missionaries

The main hospital street

and twelve rowers at four o'clock one misty morning. When the boat swung out of the side channel into the main stream, dawn was breaking. There was no sound other than the splash of oars, the songs of the rowers and those of the birds.

Suddenly the rowers stopped singing. Through the mist they could see a herd of hippopotamuses moving towards the boat. They were almost as tall as a man, and twice as long as they were tall. The rowers pulled in nearer the bank, where the current was not so strong and they could move more quickly. Even there they knew the dangers. Pythons might drop from the branches above them.

All was well this time, but it was not always so. Dr Schweitzer once told how a man was chased by a hippopotamus in Lake Sonange. The man went out with a friend to fish. When they were nearing their landing stage, a hippopotamus came up in the water and tossed their boat into the air. The friend got away but the hippopotamus chased the other man about in the water for half an hour. He had to be taken to the hospital with a broken thigh.

Although the ground on which to build the hospital was granted by the district commissioner, it was difficult to find workers. Traders were using most of the men who were willing to work, but one trader did let his workers clear the ground for the hospital. Schweitzer had to divide his time between his patients and the labourers, because these men only worked when he was with them.

He had expected to give up his music when he went to Africa. But after his busy days he found playing the piano restful. He also wrote books far into the night. When all other oil-lamps were out, his was still burning brightly. Yet he was up in time to do an hour's work before breakfast.

Less than three months after his arrival in Africa his

medical supplies began to run out. He ordered more to be sent from Europe, but it was several months before they arrived.

During his first nine months in Africa Schweitzer treated nearly 7000 patients. By that time he had built the hospital and it was in use. It was much more primitive than the hospitals in which he had worked in Europe. There was a small room where he met the patients, a room for making up the medicines, an operating-theatre, a waiting-room and the patients' wards. The patients' friends stayed with them to help and cook their food. They slept beside them on the floor. Their cooking pots were kept under the bed!

New patients waiting to see a doctor in the Lambarene hospital

Later, two special huts were built for patients who were suffering from dysentery and sleeping sickness, so that these diseases would not be passed on to all the others.

Suddenly the doctor was ordered to stop working. It was 1914, and France* was at war with Germany. Because Schweitzer and his wife were German citizens, and Gabon was a French colony, they were arrested. They were not put in jail but were kept prisoners in their own house. Native soldiers stood guard at their door to make sure that they did not go outside and mix with those under French rule.

Both European and African people were angry at having no doctor to treat them. Three months passed before they got the ban lifted and Schweitzer was allowed to treat his patients again.

For three years the work went on more or less as before, but both the doctor and his wife were very tired. In the rainy season they had to cope with floods. Food and medical supplies began to run short. Because of the war, friends in Europe were unable to send money, and Schweitzer had to borrow to buy what was needed.

Then their work was stopped again. They were ordered by the French Government to return to Europe as prisoners of war. It was a sad day when the hospital was left without a doctor. They were both unwell when they arrived in Europe, and the cold November weather did not suit them after the heat of Africa. However a doctor was needed in the prison camp, so Schweitzer did have more freedom than other prisoners.

When peace was declared the following year, the Schweitzers did not return at once to Africa. The doctor had to get well and earn some money. Then they had a baby daughter, named Rhena.

By this time Schweitzer was famous all over Europe. For

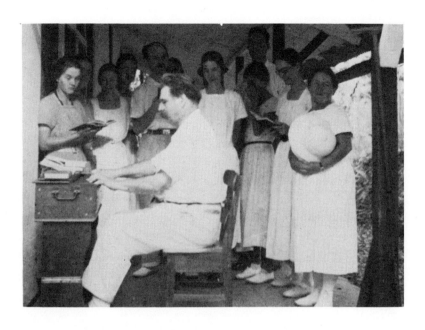

Schweitzer accompanying the hospital staff on the harmonium early one morning while they sing a birthday song for one of the doctors

years he had been known for his music, his books and his speaking ability. Now he had even greater fame because he had given up so much to do such good work in Africa. Honours and awards were given to him, and he became one of the most popular and admired men of his time. An American newspaper article described him as "the greatest man in the world!" Many people, in many countries, agreed that he was. Few men could have done so much for others in so short a time.

Letters from well-wishers and money for his work in Africa poured in. Soon he had enough to pay what he owed and was ready to continue his work among the sick people in Africa. Because his wife now had a child to care for, and the climate of Africa was not good for the health of mother and daughter, the doctor had to return alone.

The timber frame of the new pharmacy building, which was completed in 1927

Building — always building

Patients began to arrive as soon as the doctor returned. In his absence the missionaries who were left in Africa had neither the workers nor the materials to keep the hospital in good condition. It was the rainy season and a lot of help was needed to repair roofs and rebuild part of the hospital. The jungle had spread into the mission grounds and this had to be cleared.

One of the greatest trials at this time was the people of the Benjabi tribe. They were small people who lived in the middle of the jungle. They came to the hospital hungry, and wearing no clothes. Their tribal marks were cut deep into their faces and they looked what they were — true savages.

They took whatever they wanted, no matter to whom it belonged. They even took the food of sick patients who were too ill to prevent them. They spoke a language which no

17

one understood, and were gloomy and unfriendly. Many Benjabis were brought to the hospital after the witch-doctor had failed to cure them. Some were scared of what the white doctor might do to them.

Dysentery spread because friends of the patients would not stay away. The rain continued to make holes in the roofs, and iron roofing material had to be ordered from Europe to repair them.

Then came famine, which lasted for months. A lot of rain had fallen in the dry season the previous year, and this had kept the people from planting their crops. Many Africans were so hungry and weak that they sat in their huts and waited to die. Schweitzer had bought a lot of rice, but by the time his patients were fed there was not much left to give to others.

Added to all this, he found that the site on which he had built the hospital was unhealthy and had become too cramped. There was not enough space to prevent the spread of disease. Many people would have felt the task was hopeless and would have given up.

But Schweitzer knew he must go on, and find a larger and more healthy site. He said nothing about his decision until he had been given permission, by the Gabon Government, to build on a site of 68 hectares. This site was big enough to build a village in which those suffering from leprosy could live and work. On another part of the ground the new hospital could be built for 400 patients. There would be plenty of room for more buildings as the need arose. That would still leave a big piece of ground to grow fruit and vegetables. Never again would they suffer a famine.

A dream come true

The jungle had to be cleared before building could begin, but the doctor and his helpers began to make plans.

18

The buildings would be stronger. There would be no more bamboo huts with leaking roofs. They would make a wooden framework and fix a strong length of iron at each end. The sides of the buildings could be left open, with wire netting to keep out mosquitoes and other insects.

Patients could be kept apart, so that others should not catch their illnesses. They would be better housed, and there would be a suitable building for mental patients.

Patients' friends were given their tasks. Every morning they lined up to be told what they had to do. Then they were given their tools.

Clearing the jungle was a dangerous job. Pythons lurked in the trees. Leopards and gorillas were living in the forest. Lizards and frogs, which were not dangerous, were carefully moved out of the way by the doctor to save them from being trodden on.

In January 1927, the building was finished. With great joy all the supplies and equipment from the old hospital were taken upstream, and the patients moved into the new hospital.

Later that evening, when Schweitzer looked round the hospital, people said: "It's a good hut, doctor. A very good hut."

More doctors and nurses arrived from Europe. With their help, people who were too ill to come to the hospital could be visited in their villages.

Now Schweitzer was able to take some more trips home, partly for fund raising and partly to see his family. His home was now in two places — Europe and Africa.

When he arrived in Europe he was welcomed as a hero. Everywhere people filled the halls where he was to speak or play the organ. It was the same on each visit he made during his long life. His time was as fully occupied in Europe as it was in Africa.

In 1952 he was awarded the Nobel Peace Prize. This is a prize of a large sum of money given every year by the Norwegian Government. It is awarded to the man or woman who has done most for the cause of peace and brotherhood throughout the world. Schweitzer went to Oslo, in Norway, to collect the award.

With this money he was able to realise his dream to build a special village for 300 people suffering from leprosy. It

The village for leprosy patients, called "the village of light"

was built on a hill above the hospital. Many people have been cured there and have returned to their own villages. One man who had been cured earlier was so happy that he stayed to help build the village. There is a school for the children where the teacher suffers from leprosy.

In October 1955, Schweitzer came to England to receive the Order of Merit from the Queen. He was only the second person from overseas to be given this award.

Eight years later Ali Silver, one of the helpers, described life at the hospital founded and built by Schweitzer in Africa. She wrote:

We live and work in trust and confidence. When necessary, doctors and nurses work day and night without thinking about time. The patients have freedom throughout the hospital. They fish in the river, they take their firewood from the forest, they eat all they wish of the fruits which are grown. Everything is free for them. Children are playing everywhere, the little ones, often completely naked, enjoying the sun on the waters of the Ogowe River. The animals know that they can live in security here. They are not killed for food, and when they die they die a natural death.

Schweitzer, with his love of animals, would not allow any of those kept in the hospital grounds to be killed for food.

Albert Schweitzer had given a lot to this part of Africa. He had built a good hospital for the people, had cured many of their diseases, and made them happy. His patients and staff called him "the great doctor". Now the people could do without the witch-doctors and their charms. The great doctor had done what he came to Africa to do. He had shown them a better way.

Sunday was a day when no work was done which could

possibly be left for another day. A bell was rung to call everyone who wished to come to morning service. One service was held in the leper village for patients unable to walk. Another was in the main hospital area. Schweitzer went to both. He played the "little harmonium" until everyone arrived. Then he talked about Jesus and his love. He spoke simply about the things his listeners could understand. He said of his preaching: "If someone only hears me once, he has at least a hint of what it means to be a Christian."

In 1955 a Cambridge professor said: "In all humility let us salute this faithful soldier of Christ, seeing in him an example of Christian charity long to be remembered."

A year before he died Schweitzer was able to say that over a thousand people were housed and fed at the hospital each day. Besides patients and their families there were six doctors and thirty-five European nurses. Yet there were still over 200 patients for whom there was no room, and still more building to be done.

A good road had been built and patients could be brought in by car and hospital lorry.

Albert Schweitzer died on 4 September 1965 at the age of ninety, in the hospital which he had built and loved.

BIOGRAPHICAL NOTES

Albert Schweitzer was born on 14 January 1875, in a Lutheran vicarage in Kaysersberg, in Upper Alsace, where his father was pastor. When Albert was six months old his father became pastor at Gunsbach.

Albert early learned to play the organ and later studied philosophy and theology at the University of Strasbourg. He became a well-known authority on the music of Bach and studied music under some of the best-known musicians of the time. Besides being an organist he took an interest in old organs. He wrote many books, most of which were translated into a number of European languages.

In 1913 he graduated in medicine to enable him to go to Africa as a medical missionary. There he built a hospital and a village for people suffering from leprosy.

In addition to being given many honorary degrees he was awarded the Nobel Peace Prize in 1952. He went to England in 1955 to receive the Order of Merit from Queen Elizabeth.

As a German citizen he was imprisoned in France for three months during World War I.

He became one of the most remarkable figures of the twentieth century. More than twenty years before his death he was described on the cover of *Time* magazine as "The Greatest Man in the World".

When he was eighty the B.B.C. Panorama team went to Lambarene to prepare a programme on his life and work there.

He died on 4 September 1965, in the hospital he built at Lambarene. His daughter, Rhena, was left in charge of the hospital which he had founded, and built up over a period of fifty years.

In 1976 it was decided to completely rebuild the hospital as the old buildings had greatly deteriorated in the tropical climate. Through the combined efforts of the Gabonese Government and many friends of Lambarene in Europe and the U.S.A., a new hospital (built on a site behind the old one) was opened in January 1981. It is maintained by F.I.S.L., an international foundation which comprises representatives from Gabon and the International Association of Albert Schweitzer of Lambarene (A.I.S.L.). There are many national supporting groups; Dr Schweitzer's Hospital Fund is the British group. Donations of money and materials to help maintain the valuable healing work are sent in from all over the world, and each year hundreds of people from many countries visit the hospital.

THINGS TO DO

A Test yourself

Here are some short questions. See if you can remember the answers from what you have read. Then write them down in a few words.

1 What did Albert Schweitzer do to be like the village boys?
2 When did he start playing the organ?
3 How old was he when he went to Africa?
4 What did the Africans buy from the witch-doctors?
5 How did Schweitzer travel to Africa?
6 What did he use for a hospital at first?
7 What insects are mentioned in the story?
8 Dr Schweitzer built two hospitals. Why did he build the second?
9 Name some of the illnesses which Dr Schweitzer treated.
10 How old was Schweitzer when he died?

B Think through

These questions need longer answers. Think about them, and then try to write two or three sentences in answer to each one. You may look up the story again to help you.

1 How did Schweitzer show his feelings for all living things?
2 What were some of the problems the doctor had to face when he got to Africa?
3 Separate buildings were put up for some patients. Why was this necessary?
4 The hospital in Africa was different from those in this country. What were the differences?

C Talk about

Here are some questions for you to talk about with each other. Try to give reasons for what you say or think. Try to find out the different opinions which people have about such questions.

1 Why do you think the schoolboys thought Albert Schweitzer was different from them?
2 Albert Schweitzer felt he had to go to Africa as a doctor. What made him decide to go?
3 Do you think he could have done better staying at home?

25

4 The doctor's patients called him "the great doctor". Others said he was the greatest man in the world. Why do you think they said that?

D Find out

Choose one or two of the subjects below and find out all you can about them. History books, geography books and newspapers may be useful. Perhaps you can also use reference books in your library to look up some of the names and places.

1 Find out all you can about driver ants and other tropical creatures such as pythons, hippos and elephants.
2 Find out all you can about Lambarene today and other medical missions. You could write to one of the missionary societies about this, or contact the Treasurer and Secretary of Dr Schweitzer's Hospital Fund.
3 What were the dates of the First World War and which countries were at war? How did it end and when?
4 Copy the map on page 5. How far did people from the other settlements have to travel to reach Schweitzer's hospital? (Remember it was easiest to travel by river.)
5 Find out all you can about Africa today, especially central Africa.

USEFUL INFORMATION

Addresses

Dr Schweitzer's Hospital Fund (A Registered Charity)
F. G. Torrie Attwell, Hon. Treasurer and Secretary
156 Cheston Avenue
Croydon
Surrey CRo 8DD.

(British Committee: Chairman, J. R. Witchalls, M.B., B.S.; J. Braba-
zon; S. G. Browne, C.M.G.; Prof. L. Bruce-Chwatt, C.M.G.; P. F. E.
Mark, A.R.I.B.A.; Mrs V. Mark; Miss Nancy Martin; Rev. Dr C. M.
Morris; F. A. W. Schweitzer, M.S., F.R.C.S.; Prof. A. W. Woodruff,
C.M.G.)

These are societies which can give information about medical missions
today:

The Baptist Missionary Society
93 Gloucester Place
London W1H 4AA.

The Church Missionary Society
157 Waterloo Road
London SE1 8UU.

The Methodist Church Overseas Division
25 Marylebone Road
London NW1 5JB.

N.B. Remember to enclose a stamped addressed envelope for the reply.
A postal order for 50p would also be helpful if you want plenty of
material.

More books to read

Albert Schweitzer, a Biography, by James Brabazon (Gollancz).
All Men Are Brothers, by Charlie May Simon (Blackie).
Memoirs of Childhood and Youth, by Albert Schweitzer (Allen & Unwin).
More from the Primeval Forest, by Albert Schweitzer (A. & C. Black).
On the Edge of the Primeval Forest, by Albert Schweitzer (A. & C. Black).
Pears Cyclopaedia and other encyclopedias for details about insects and animals mentioned.
Schweitzer, by George Marshall and David Billing (George Bles).

While these books are intended for adult readers, parts could be read by pupils under the teacher's guidance.

Filmstrip

Albert Schweitzer (CP 32). Available from Church Army Filmstrips, 5 Cosway Street, London NW1 5NR.